Disney · PIXAR
INSIDE OUT

THE ESSENTIAL GUIDE

Written by **Steve Bynghall**

Contents

Introduction

Have you ever wondered what goes on inside someone's head? If you looked inside Riley Andersen's mind you'd find The Five Emotions guiding her through life: Joy, Sadness, Anger and Disgust, as well as many other inhabitants. They all work day and night inside Riley's mind. They sort her thoughts, manage her memories, give her ideas and produce her dreams. So far, the Emotions are doing a great job. Riley is a happy and healthy 11-year-old growing up in Minnesota. But there are big challenges ahead as Riley's family moves to San Francisco. Can the Emotions cope with all the change?

Riley

Riley Andersen is an ordinary, happy, 11-year-old girl who loves her family, her friends and her favourite game of ice hockey. Not too much riles Riley – she's positive and bright – and spends most of her time smiling. But when life starts to get more complicated, Riley's personality starts to change!

Cry baby
When Riley was born she was a bundle of joy. She was quiet and content… for about 30 seconds, until she started bawling at the top of her lungs!

Life of Riley
Strength: Riley's positive attitude means she gets on very well with everybody.

❋ ❋ ❋

Weakness: Riley isn't used to big changes in her life and doesn't know how to react.

Going for the goal
Just like her sports-mad Dad, Riley is totally hooked on ice hockey. She is passionate about playing for her team, the Prairie Dogs. Riley's had plenty of practice – she has been scoring goals on the ice since she was a little girl.

Wide-eyed and cheerful expression

Did you know?
In Minnesota, Riley goes ice skating on her local lake whenever it freezes over.

"I'm kinda nervous, but I'm mostly excited!"

Amazing imagination

From a bright pink imaginary friend named Bing Bong to a volcano spitting lava in her living room, Riley has always had a very vivid imagination. Her highly active mind means that even the most mundane day can be transformed into an exciting adventure!

Home in Minnesota

Riley has grown up in a comfortable house in Minnesota. She loves her home and has never lived anywhere else…

Scuffed trainers

Best friends

Riley's lifelong best friend is Meg. They've been laughing together ever since they were little. Once Meg made Riley laugh so hard that milk actually came out of her nose!

Joy

As the most optimistic of the Emotions, Joy is always happy and hopeful. With her sunny outlook she is able to see the positive in everything. Joy never gives up on her aim to make Riley happy every single day. So far, she has been pretty successful!

Joy enjoys

Joy loves special golden memories, joking around and group hugs. But more than anything, she adores Riley's smile.

Pride and Joy

Because all the Emotions want Riley to be happy, Joy is usually the one at the controls. She is very proud that Riley has so many happy memories.

Head Emotion

As their unofficial leader, Joy keeps the other Emotions organised and on track. While they are very glad Joy's in charge, she can be a little bossy sometimes!

Life of Riley

Positive: Joy has made sure Riley has had a very happy childhood.

Negative: Joy doesn't realise it's natural for Riley to sometimes feel sad.

"I've got a great idea!"

Glowing, golden
memory sphere

Did you know?
Joy was the first Emotion to arrive at Headquarters after Riley was born.

Positive plans

Joy works very hard to try and keep Riley cheerful. She watches carefully for warning signs of potential trouble around the corner. Just in case things go wrong, she always has a backup plan!

Merry music

Joy relaxes by playing the accordion. Although she doesn't think of it as playing so much as hugging! But her musical efforts aren't enjoyed by the other Emotions!

Always likes to
be barefoot

Cheerful,
flowery dress

Sadness

Sadness often finds herself feeling thoroughly miserable. In fact, this moping Emotion can find a cause for sorrow in even the happiest of happenings in Riley's world. She would like to be more positive… but how can she when life is so awful?

Years of tears

Throughout Riley's young life, there have been many seriously upsetting incidents – such as spilled ice cream! With Sadness in charge the tears just keep rolling.

Tearful not cheerful

Joy is always trying to get Sadness to look on the bright side – without success! When her efforts fail, Joy puts the miserable Emotion in a Circle of Sadness and tells her to stay inside. That way she can't spread her gloominess.

Downbeat reading

In her spare time, Sadness has read many of the mind manuals in Headquarters. Unfortunately, Long Term Memory Retrieval Volume 47 is very unlikely to raise a smile.

Negative touch

Sadness has a habit of turning the brightest moments into gloomy situations. Each time she touches one of Riley's happy memories it turns sad and blue.

Sombre expression

"It's like I'm having a breakdown!"

Weepy world

Sadness doesn't want to feel down all the time but she just can't seem to help it. There is so much to weep about in the world, from losing toys to watching sandcastles collapse!

Life of Riley

Positive: Sadness has actually helped Riley feel better after a good cry.

✳ ✳ ✳

Negative: If Sadness is in charge of the console, Riley's day can be drenched by tears.

Sadness is always blue - in colour and in mood.

Fear

Fear is frightened of almost everything, but he is proud that by being constantly scared he has saved Riley from the perils of the world. Fear does feel shaky most of the time, but you won't shake him from his belief that ultra-cautious is the only way to be.

Eyes wide open in shock

100% non-scary knitwear

Legs often used for running away

In a flap

It's easy for Fear to let things get on top of him. Thankfully Joy is there to calm him down when he is feeling trembly.

Life of Riley

Positive: Fear is always aware of what's around, so Riley doesn't trip or hurt herself.

Negative: Fear's worries can make Riley feel nervous in situations that don't have to be scary.

Scare care

None of the other Emotions understand how dangerous the world can be! Fear believes that being scared is not necessarily a bad thing. Whenever Riley feels scared, she pays attention to her surroundings and is extra careful, which keeps her safe.

Fear in charge

Fear is always on the lookout for potential hazards, such as low-hanging power cords. Over the years he has saved Riley from some pretty nasty accidents.

"I'm so jumpy! My nerves are shot."

Nervous wreck

After arriving in San Francisco and hearing about the area's earthquakes, Fear is even more jumpy than usual. Now even the slightest surprise reduces him to a trembling mess.

Quitter

When the going gets tough inside Headquarters, Fear tries to run away. Yes, it may be the coward's way out but he thinks at least he'll be the coward who survives!

13

Anger

Anger has some serious issues with his bad temper. He gets absolutely furious every time he thinks things are not fair for Riley. This overreacting Emotion believes in justice, but he also believes in screaming, shouting and throwing chairs!

"Now for a few well-placed withering scowls!"

Anger management

Anger tries to relax by reading the newspaper, but it doesn't usually work. If the headlines don't cause outrage, then something he overhears will!

Think second

Anger is always impatient and impulsive. His reaction to feeling frustrated is to fight first and think second. While problems may be quickly resolved, it also leads to trouble and tantrums!

Teeth gritted in frustration

Tie with red, angry design

Hot head

When Anger reaches his boiling point, bright flames shoot out of his head! The other Emotions have sometimes had to use an extinguisher to put out his fires!

All the rage

When Anger is at the console, Riley becomes pretty irritable. You can expect rude remarks, a whole lot of rash decisions and plenty of melodrama!

Anger's idea

Anger is not usually a smiley kind of a guy. However, when he picks out an idea bulb, for once he is pleased rather than peeved. He is sure that this will help fix all of Riley's problems.

Did you know?

Anger is dying to try out any new swear words he learns as Riley grows up.

Disgust

Disgust believes that the world is riddled with foul odours, toxic tastes and poisonous people (mainly boys). With so much dirt, disease and bad fashion sense in Riley's world, Disgust has made it her mission to keep Riley safe by warning her of every possible poison.

In control

When danger looms, Disgust is always ready to grab the controls. Her quick thinking has saved Riley from many disgusting incidents!

Difficult attitude

With her strong opinions and attitude, Disgust can come across as abrupt and aloof. Thankfully the other Emotions are quite used to her sarcastic tone!

Revolting

Ever since Riley was a baby, Disgust has protected her from the world's most vile vegetable – broccoli! Anything that smells that bad can't be good for her.

"I'm gonna be sick..."

Lips curled into a sneer

Did you know?

Disgust thinks that cities are horrible, dirty places – they should always be avoided!

Always right

Disgust sticks to strict beliefs about what food should look like or which clothes are uncool. That's because she views her own great taste as a gift – one that has saved Riley from being grossed-out on many occasions.

For Riley

Like all of the Emotions, Disgust always has Riley's best interests at heart. As she watches the view screen in Headquarters, it is obvious just how much she cares.

Fashionable pink shoes

Life of Riley

Positive: Disgust keeps Riley from being poisoned – both physically and socially.

❋ ❋ ❋

Negative: Thanks to Disgust, Riley misses out on nutritious broccoli.

17

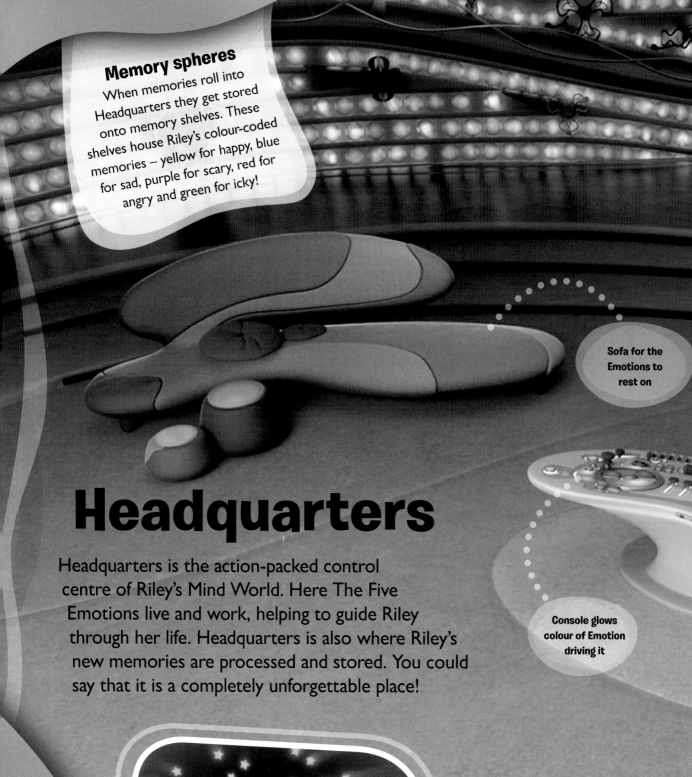

Memory spheres

When memories roll into Headquarters they get stored onto memory shelves. These shelves house Riley's colour-coded memories – yellow for happy, blue for sad, purple for scary, red for angry and green for icky!

Sofa for the Emotions to rest on

Headquarters

Headquarters is the action-packed control centre of Riley's Mind World. Here The Five Emotions live and work, helping to guide Riley through her life. Headquarters is also where Riley's new memories are processed and stored. You could say that it is a completely unforgettable place!

Console glows colour of Emotion driving it

Viewing screen

The viewing screen allows the Emotions to see exactly what Riley is seeing at any time. Joy loves to watch the glowing star stickers on Riley's bedroom ceiling at night.

Core memory holder stored beneath the floor

Core memory holder

When Riley experiences a life-changing event, a core memory sphere is formed. It rolls into Headquarters and is stored in the core memory holder. These powerful memories power the Islands of Personality, which make Riley who she is.

Console and comfort

The complicated console has lots of buttons, levers and dials. "Driving" the console can be very hard work for the Emotions. Thankfully there are comfortable seats nearby to relax on.

Power tower

Headquarters towers above the rest of the Mind World. The high-rise home of the Emotions gives off a glowing white light – a symbol of its power and importance.

Mum and Dad

In many ways, Jill and Bill Andersen are the perfect parents. They are proud of their daughter and have given their only child a happy and loving childhood. But Riley is growing up fast. She won't be their happy-go-lucky little girl forever. Life is definitely about to get a lot more interesting for this family!

"Yay! Nice job Riley!"

Fashionable red glasses

Tied-back hair shows she means business!

Happy families

Riley has many magical memories of happy times with her parents. Joy loves them; she's always re-running her favourite family memories on the view screen.

Did you know?
Mum's Emotions all wear red glasses and Dad's Emotions all have moustaches.

Hockey mum

Riley's mum is her daughter's biggest supporter. At every ice hockey game, she's there rooting for Riley and cheering her on from the sidelines.

"Come back here! You little monkey!"

Big, goofy smile

Sand man

Riley's dad is a really good sport. He's even allowed Riley to bury him in the sand at the beach. It's lucky she stopped at his neck!

Mum and Dad's dream

Riley's parents both have a sense of adventure. Dad has always dreamed of starting his own company in San Francisco and Mum shares his excitement about a new start in a new city.

Sensible business clothes

Family fun

The Andersens love goofing about and making each other laugh. They can't imagine any problem they couldn't overcome with a bit of fun family time.

Life of Riley

Positive: Mum and Dad have given Riley a wonderful childhood.

Negative: Riley's parents don't realise what a big change moving to San Francisco is for her.

21

Islands of Personality

The five Islands of Personality help to define who Riley is. They have grown as she has grown up. Family, Honesty, Hockey, Friendship and Goofball Islands each represent something that is very important to Riley and has become a key part of her character.

Recall tube

Riley always tries to be truthful. Welcome to Honesty Island!

Statue of Riley being hugged by Mum and Dad on Family Island.

Lightline stretches from core memory holder to Family Island

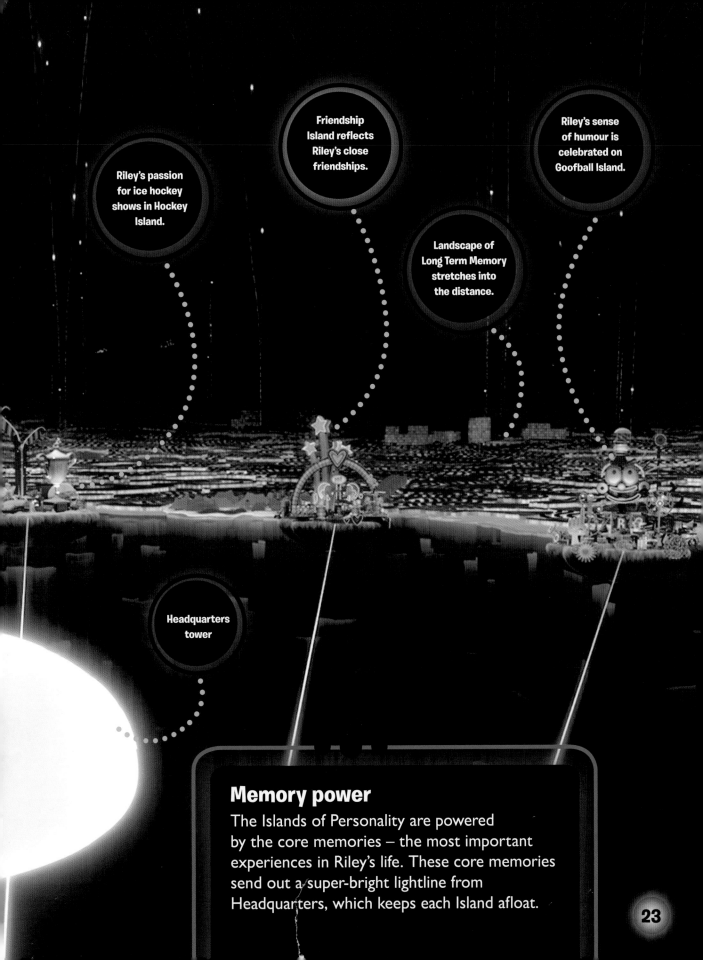

Riley's passion for ice hockey shows in Hockey Island.

Friendship Island reflects Riley's close friendships.

Riley's sense of humour is celebrated on Goofball Island.

Landscape of Long Term Memory stretches into the distance.

Headquarters tower

Memory power

The Islands of Personality are powered by the core memories – the most important experiences in Riley's life. These core memories send out a super-bright lightline from Headquarters, which keeps each Island afloat.

Memory Guide

Memories are very important in the Mind World. They are a major influence on Riley's mood, personality and behaviour. But how do they get formed and why are some memories more powerful? Here is a simple guide to explain how memories are made and played, and how some stay strong while others are forgotten forever!

Memories made

Whenever Riley experiences something, such as ice skating on the lake with her family, a brand new memory is made.

On the shelf

Each new memory is a bright, glowing sphere which rolls down a tube into Headquarters. Most memories are stored on shelves in Headquarters until Riley goes to sleep each night.

Colour coded

Each memory is coloured according to which Emotion helped to create it. Happy memories are yellow, sad ones are blue, scary ones are purple, angry ones are red and gross ones are green.

Core memories

Very important memories are stored in the core memory holder in Headquarters. Core memories can last a lifetime!

Long Term Memory

A labyrinth of Long Term Memory shelves stores all of Riley's memory spheres. The Forgetters remove memories to make space for new ones.

Random memories

The Forgetters like to play pranks by sending up odd memories to Headquarters. That's why Riley suddenly remembers a catchy chewing gum advertisement!

Memory Dump

The Forgetters send old memories to the Memory Dump. This is more than a dump – it is an ever-multiplying, massive mountain of memories! There's no going back for any memories that end up here.

Recall tube

While Riley sleeps, the Emotions activate a button on the floor that sends all of the memories from the shelves up a tube to Long Term Memory. The tube is also used to recall memories from Long Term storage to be played again.

Islands of Personality

Each core memory powers an Island of Personality, which is connected to Headquarters by a lightline.

On the Road

Moving from Minnesota to California means a very long drive for the Andersens! The road trip to San Francisco takes Riley and her family from the chill of the Midwest to the warmth of the Pacific Coast, and through different time zones. It also takes them to a very different way of life!

Moving on

Selling their home in Minnesota is a big step for Riley's family. Riley is sad to leave the familiarity of the home she grew up in, but she's trying really hard to stay positive.

Desert drive

The drive across America takes a really, really long time! The Andersens' heavily loaded car travels through endless cornfields, craggy mountains and the scorching heat of the desert.

Daydreamer

In the car, Riley daydreams about what her new home might look like. Perhaps a giant edible gingerbread house covered in sweets is unlikely...

Sightseeing

There is a lot to take in on the journey. Seeing the tall buildings of San Francisco fills Riley with both excitement and nerves about her new adventure.

The final stretch

Everybody is excited as the Andersens drive the final stretch of their journey. The bay and the skyline of San Francisco look amazing! However, the Emotions are disappointed to find the Golden Gate Bridge isn't actually made of solid gold!

Peeling paintwork

Room for improvement
Inside, the house is dirty, murky and run down. Even worse, the van with the family's furniture hasn't arrived yet!

Dark and empty rooms

Walls coated with grime

First impressions
From the outside, the new house is narrow and uninviting. Climbing the stairs to her new home, Riley discovers rotten woodwork and peeling paint… and that's not appealing at all!

New Home
On the drive to San Francisco, Riley is excited about her new home. Will it be as wonderful as she imagined in her daydreams? But when Riley arrives she's shocked to find that the house is far from fantastic! It's definitely a world away from the cosy home she left behind in Minnesota.

Hard night

Riley is also disappointed to find her bedroom is pretty dreary. Since her furniture hasn't arrived yet, poor Riley has to spend her first night in San Francisco sleeping on the hard floor.

Bad pizza

Not even her new local pizza place can provide a reason for Riley to smile. Each slice is covered in beastly broccoli – and that's the only pizza on the menu!

First Day

Riley's first day in her new school is nerve-racking. Joy has prepared a plan to cope with tricky situations, such as being singled out by the teacher. Sadly things don't go well! The Emotions find themselves facing a crisis as Riley cries in front of her entire class!

Surprised student

Riley's new school books

30

Feeling blue
Joy tells Sadness to keep well away from the memories. However, when Sadness touches a happy memory it changes colour to a sad blue, triggering Riley's tears.

Unable to look away!

Sob story
When the teacher asks Riley about life back in Minnesota, it makes her feel sad about the world she has left behind. As tears roll down Riley's cheeks, she becomes the focus of her whispering classmates.

Drama in Headquarters

Headquarters might not exactly be an oasis of calm, but Joy usually manages to keep things under control. However, Riley's first day at school proves to be a big test for all of the Emotions. As Riley cries in her new class, a drama unfolds which results in both Joy and Sadness leaving the safety of Headquarters!

Console left unattended

Horrified Emotions watch Joy and Sadness disappear

Shocked Emotions

Anger, Fear and Disgust are shocked to see Sadness and Joy and all the core memories get sucked up the recall tube, out of Headquarters. The three Emotions are on their own now, and must do their best to help steer Riley through this crisis.

Blue memory

When Riley stands up to introduce herself to the class, Sadness touches a happy memory and it turns blue! The Emotions start to panic about how Riley might react.

Core memory misery

Riley cries in front of all her classmates, creating a new sad core memory! The Emotions go into meltdown because Riley has only ever had happy core memories before.

Emotional struggle

Joy tries to stop the blue core memory from being stored in the holder, but Sadness wants her memory to stay! The two Emotions struggle and crash into the holder, knocking out all of the core memories.

Out of here

In the chaos, the core memories get sucked up the recall tube! Joy and Sadness try desperately to stop them from being lost forever, but the two Emotions end up being sucked up the tube and into the Mind World, too!

Protecting memories

Joy is determined to get back to Headquarters with Riley's core memories intact – she knows Riley will never be herself without them! Now Joy just has to find a way out of this crazy Mind World…

Shelves stacked high with memories

Train of Thought

Imagination Land

The most colourful corner of the Mind World is Imagination Land. Here Riley's imagination has run riot to create everything from a French Fry Forest to a town made of clouds! There's even an Imaginary Boyfriend Generator!

Train tracks appear in front of the train and disappear behind it.

Long Term Memory

Long Term Memory is an endless maze of gigantic shelves containing millions of memory spheres. The spectacular landscape might be unforgettable, but it is also very easy to get lost in this labyrinth!

Abstract Thought

The weirdest place in the Mind World must be Abstract Thought. Anybody who visits gets twisted, distorted and deconstructed. It is not a good look for Joy and Sadness!

Preschool World

Located in Imagination Land, Preschool World is home to Graham Cracker Castle, Sparkle Pony Mountain, Princess Dream World and Stuffed Animal Hall of Fame. But now that Riley is growing up, these areas are being bulldozed!

Mind World

It is hard to get your head around what an amazing place the Mind World is! Each astonishing area is a unique place where a part of Riley's thinking happens. It is not only vast, but also constantly changing. To Joy and Sadness it looks more than a little overwhelming!

Bing Bong

Fun-loving Bing Bong was once Riley's imaginary friend. They used to play together all the time. But ever since Riley turned four, her cuddly companion has been without a job and playmate. Now he's determined to get back to being Riley's best friend again!

Funny friend

Riley imagined Bing Bong into life as a funny-looking creature who was part cat, part elephant and part dolphin. Bing Bong would give anything to have his old pal back.

Way back

When Bing Bong bumps into Joy and Sadness in Long Term Memory, he vows to help them find their way back to Headquarters. He hopes Joy can help Riley to remember him, too.

Dream drama

In a desperate bid to be remembered by Riley, Bing Bong boldly sneaks into a scene in one of her dreams. He just wants to get noticed!

Did you know?

Bing Bong's caramel tears taste the best!

Imaginary mayhem

Riley and Bing Bong enjoyed hours of crazy games. These included time travel and races on the ceiling! But best of all were the trips in Bing Bong's song-powered wagon rocket.

Bright pink elephant trunk

Life of Riley

Positive: When Riley was younger, Bing Bong brought joy and fun into her life.

❋ ❋ ❋

Negative: Bing Bong's crazy antics couldn't keep Riley entertained as she grew older.

Signature fingerless mittens

Body made of candy floss

Sweet tears

This sweet-natured creature cries tears of caramels and leaves a trail of them wherever he goes. It makes it quite easy to track him down!

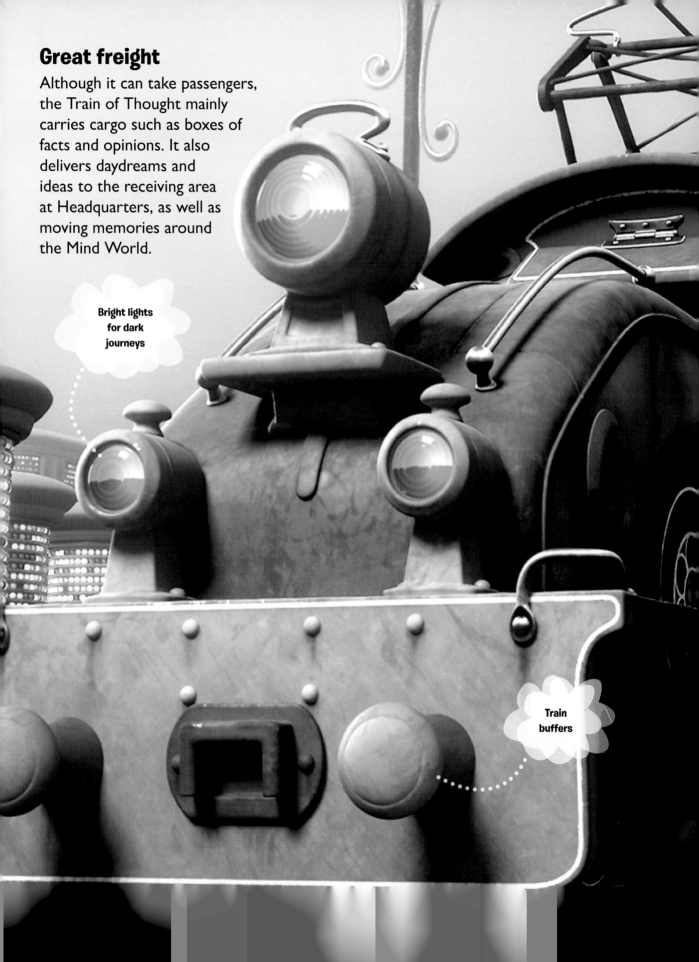

Great freight

Although it can take passengers, the Train of Thought mainly carries cargo such as boxes of facts and opinions. It also delivers daydreams and ideas to the receiving area at Headquarters, as well as moving memories around the Mind World.

Bright lights for dark journeys

Train buffers

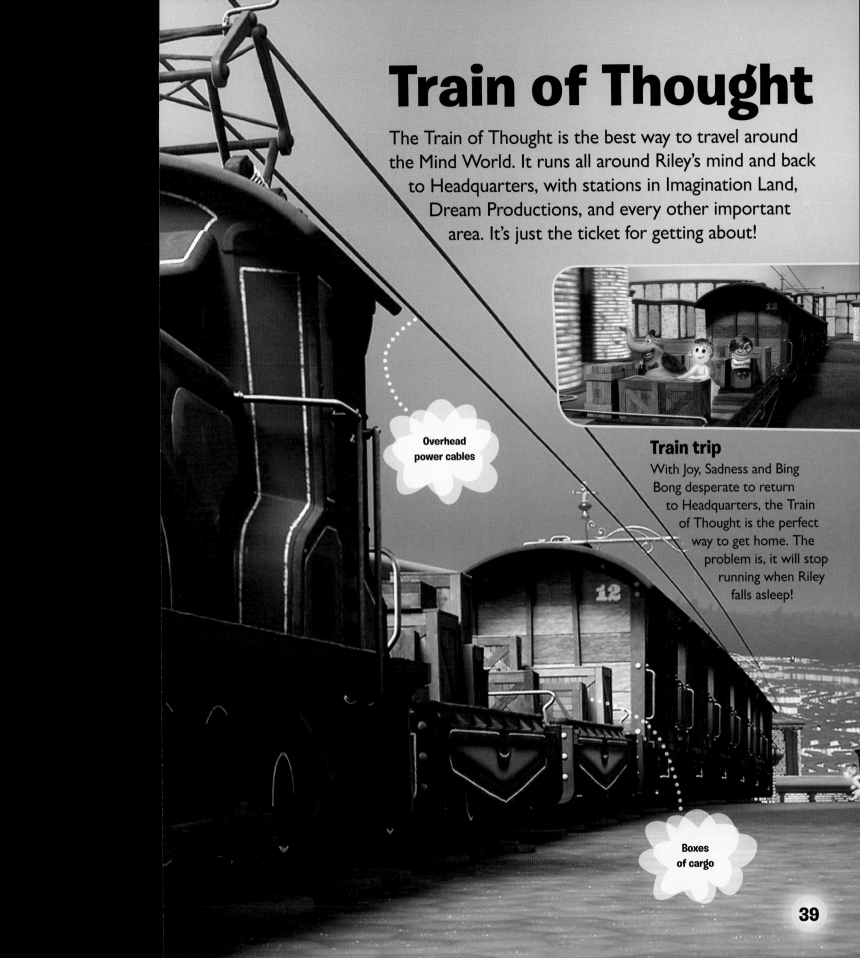

Train of Thought

The Train of Thought is the best way to travel around the Mind World. It runs all around Riley's mind and back to Headquarters, with stations in Imagination Land, Dream Productions, and every other important area. It's just the ticket for getting about!

Overhead power cables

Train trip

With Joy, Sadness and Bing Bong desperate to return to Headquarters, the Train of Thought is the perfect way to get home. The problem is, it will stop running when Riley falls asleep!

Boxes of cargo

Dream Productions

Dream Productions is where all of Riley's dreams are made. Every night a huge cast and crew create dozens of dreams on the movie-like set. The Production team works on a very tight schedule to produce live dreams. It is a lot of pressure – but there can be no mistakes!

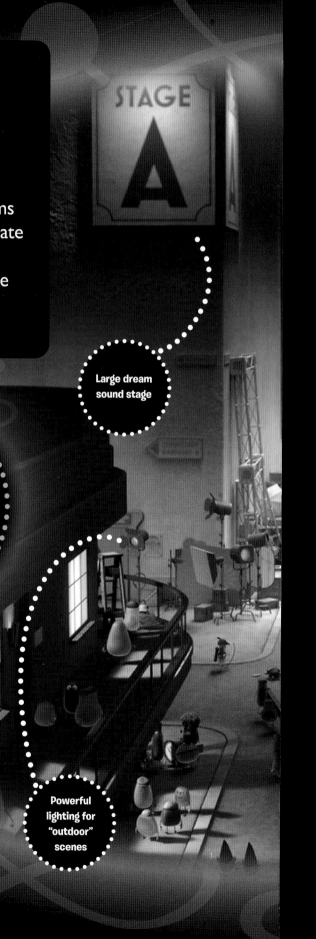

Large dream sound stage

Golden entrance
The Dream Productions entrance is the gateway to a grand and glamorous world. Behind the gates, the studio lot is buzzing with activity.

Dream team
Whether working on a magical adventure or a serious drama, Dream Productions always delivers. The stars may get all the attention, but the incredible crew behind the scenes is just as important. These assistants, camera operators and directors are always very busy on set.

Powerful lighting for "outdoor" scenes

Reality check

The secret to the success of the dreams is a reality filter – a special lens that covers the camera and makes Riley's dreams appear real to her.

Posters showing previous dreams

Cringe!

Dreams are often written to reflect the events of the day. So when Riley has a terrible day at school, that night's dreams will capture some of the cringeworthy classroom moments.

Subconscious

When Bing Bong is arrested for troublemaking in Dream Productions he is sent to the darkest and most dangerous area of the Mind World – the Subconscious! Here all of Riley's deepest fears and nightmares lurk in a murky maze of terrifying passages.

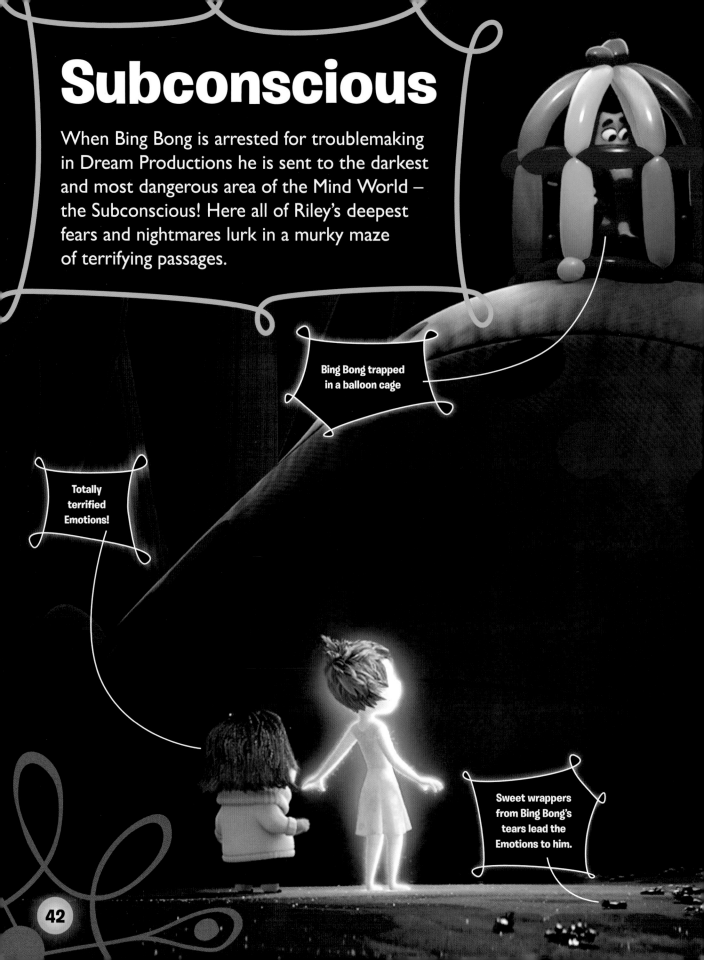

Bing Bong trapped in a balloon cage

Totally terrified Emotions!

Sweet wrappers from Bing Bong's tears lead the Emotions to him.

Frightful nightmares found in the Subconscious:

✿ Grandma's ghastly vacuum cleaner, ready to suck up all that gets in its way!

✿ The spine-chilling stairs that lead to the even spookier basement…

✿ Broccoli, the foul and fearsome food that makes Riley retch!

✿ Jangles, a giant clown who once scared Riley at a birthday party.

Jangles whispers "Who's the birthday girl?" in his sleep.

Rescue squad

Bing Bong is trapped in a cage made out of horrible squeaky balloons, on the sleeping belly of Jangles the Clown! This is no place for the fainthearted. Can Joy summon all of her courage to climb up and rescue her friend?

Mind Workers

The Mind World is populated by an amazing army of Mind Workers who do many different jobs. From dream stars to security guards, they make sure everything is running smoothly so that Riley can function properly. There is always a lot to do – so get back to work, Mind Workers!

Memories that have started to turn grey

Valuable space to store new memories

Forgetters

The Forgetters have the important job of sorting through the memories that just aren't important. Anything not worth remembering gets sucked up into an enormous vacuum, making space on the shelves for a new set of memories. Goodbye piano lessons!

Suction tube

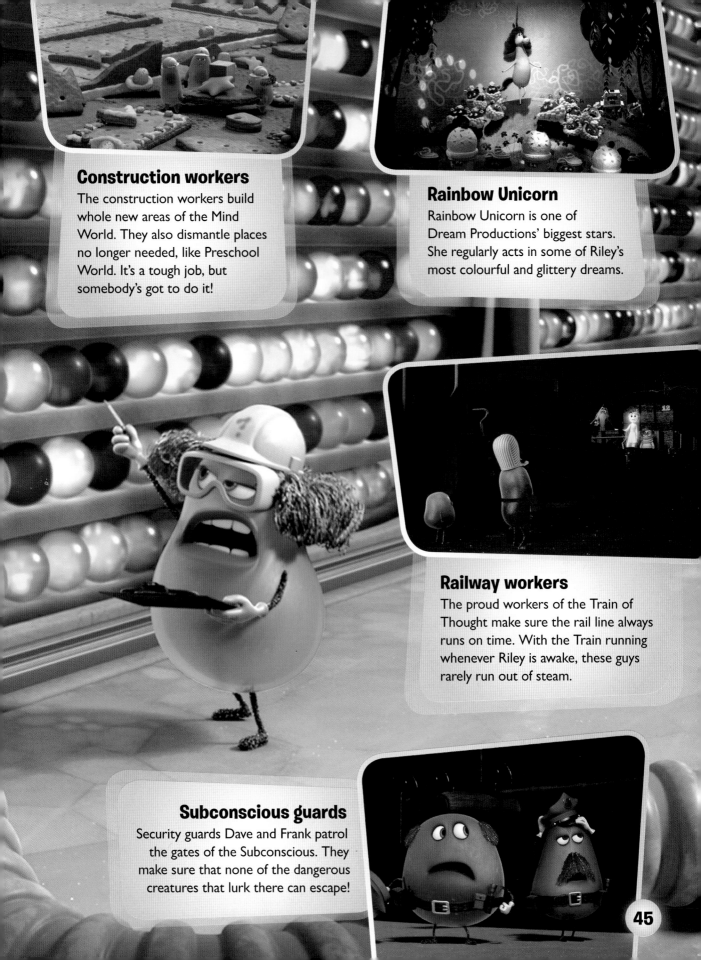

Construction workers

The construction workers build whole new areas of the Mind World. They also dismantle places no longer needed, like Preschool World. It's a tough job, but somebody's got to do it!

Rainbow Unicorn

Rainbow Unicorn is one of Dream Productions' biggest stars. She regularly acts in some of Riley's most colourful and glittery dreams.

Railway workers

The proud workers of the Train of Thought make sure the rail line always runs on time. With the Train running whenever Riley is awake, these guys rarely run out of steam.

Subconscious guards

Security guards Dave and Frank patrol the gates of the Subconscious. They make sure that none of the dangerous creatures that lurk there can escape!

Mum's Emotions

Mum's Emotions are watching the situation carefully. They all agree that they need to get Dad involved, but are less than impressed by his slow response!

Bad attitude

Usually Riley is very polite, so Mum and Dad are astonished to hear her attitude at the dinner table! They have no idea where this new behaviour has come from. What is going on with her?

Mum is great with chopsticks

Dinner Dispute

Dinner with the Andersen family is usually fun and friendly. However, this mealtime Riley has a mini-meltdown, being sarcastic with her parents and then telling them to shut up! Dad is furious with Riley's rudeness and puts his foot down, sending her straight up to her room. Dinner is a disaster!

Dad points to
Riley's room

Dinner from a
Chinese takeaway

Food fight!

With Joy and Sadness absent
from Headquarters, Anger
takes control. But his hot
temper helps the situation at
dinner quickly get out of hand!

Dad's Emotions

Dad's Emotions are all
distracted watching a hockey
game when the argument
disturbs them. When Dad is
firm with Riley they cheer as
if a player just scored a goal!

47

The Mind

The Mind Reader

INSIDE! BOOK REVIEW: LONG TERM MEMORY RETRIEVAL VOLUME 48

Issue number 4290

RILEY QUITS HOCKEY!

The whole of the Mind World was reeling today as Riley appeared to quit ice hockey forever. After a trial with new San Francisco team the Foghorns, Riley missed the puck and fell. Instead of trying again, our sports-mad girl stormed off in a huff!

TODAY'S TEMPERAMENT FORECAST OUTLOOK:
MAINLY MISERABLE

Gloom and mild despair are expected to descend in the morning and stay for the rest of the day. The afternoon may be subject to growing resentment with a 70% possibility of angry outbursts by evening time.

This temperament forecast is sponsored by Dream Productions – Where Dreams Are Made Every Day ™.

Reader

ANGER'S OFFICIAL MIND WORLD NEWSPAPER

BRAIN TRAIN: NEW TRAIN OF THOUGHT TIMETABLE REVEALED — Issue number 4288

FUTURE IS SHAKY!

Shocking new report predicts prolonged period of unhappiness for Riley

A new report issued by a think tank of Mind World workers suggests a future full of unpredictable behaviour and bad moods caused by the uncertainty of moving to San Francisco. However, a poll of readers suggests most Mind World workers think Riley will remain happy. Speaking to

The Mind Reader

Issue number 4289

INSIDE! MY GLITTERY CAREER: CELEBRITY INTERVIEW WITH DREAM STAR RAINBOW UNICORN

NO DESSERT!

"Go to your room! Now!" exclaims Dad

Last night Riley received no dessert after telling Mum and Dad to shut up at dinner time! Dad's reaction was swift as Riley got her just desserts for being rude and was sent upstairs.

Wake up, Riley!

As Joy, Sadness and Bing Bong make their way back to Headquarters, the Train of Thought they are travelling on suddenly grinds to a halt. Riley has fallen asleep! The only way to get their journey back on track is to wake Riley up. Time for a visit to Dream Productions!

Sleep signal

At Dream Productions, the sleep indicator shows when Riley is asleep. Joy watches the dial anxiously to see if her plan to wake Riley up will work!

Joy chose to be in the front - of course!

Sadness hidden in the back

Doggy dream

Joy has the idea of creating a dream so exciting that Riley will wake up! Since Riley loves dogs, Joy and Sadness dress up as a pooch and plan to enter one of her dreams.

Double trouble

Joy and Sadness' cute dog costume splits apart, but due to the reality filter, in Riley's dream the costume appears to be a real dog that has split in two. Even so, Riley stays asleep.

Bright balloons don't excite Riley awake, either!

Wake-up call

Her first idea fails, but Joy never gives up. She realises that Sadness' idea of scaring Riley awake is actually kind of a good one – and they have just stumbled across one very scary clown!

When Joy honks Jangles' nose, the terrifying clown gives chase – right into Dream Productions!

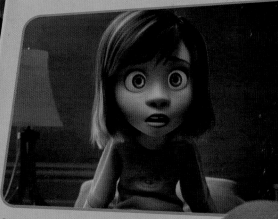

In Headquarters, Fear is on Dream Duty. Seeing Jangles makes him panic!

Overreacting, as usual, Fear wakes Riley up with a terrified jolt!

Dangerous idea

Anger is sure that if Riley can just get back to Minnesota she can make new happy core memories. He plugs in the idea to run away – problem solved!

Travel plan

Riley decides to take the bus to Minnesota. She looks online to see when the next bus is scheduled to go and finds there is one leaving the next day. Next she has to figure out how to pay for the tickets.

Running Away

Eventually, Riley gets so fed up with San Francisco that she decides to take action! It feels like everything she loves is back home in Minnesota. Riley believes the only way to be happy is to return there, but how is she going to make a journey thousands of miles away all on her own? She hatches a plan to run away.

Riley sets off to the bus station

Secret steal

While Mum is distracted, Riley finds her purse and secretly takes a credit card! This will pay for her travel. Riley has never ever stolen from her parents before. She is acting totally out of character!

No going back?

The next morning, Riley sneaks out of the house to go to the bus station without even saying goodbye! Mum and Dad think she is going to school as normal. Will Riley actually go through with her plan?

Islands Crumble

Ever since the core memories were knocked out of the memory holder, the Islands of Personality have been dark. As Riley starts to act totally out of character, each of the Islands begins to crumble and fall into the Memory Dump. The shocked Emotions realise that this is a crisis!

Rocky Hockey Island

Riley finds it hard to focus when she tries out for a new ice hockey team and she gives up! Hockey Island melts away, along with her hopes of making the team!

Family Island fades

When Mum realises that Riley is missing, she calls her daughter's mobile phone over and over again. When Riley refuses to answer, Family Island falls apart!

Farewell Friendship Island

When Riley's best friend Meg from Minnesota reveals she's made a new friend, Riley is upset and jealous. The foundations of Friendship Island crack and collapse!

Goodbye Goofball Island

Dad tries to cheer Riley up with some joking around, but she's in no mood for laughing! His monkey noises don't work like they used to and soon Goofball Island is gone!

Off goes Honesty Island

Riley's sneaky runaway scheme makes Honesty Island disappear! Will she really board the bus to Minnesota?

Flying out!

Once a memory is sent to the Memory Dump it fades away forever! It looks like Joy and Bing Bong may be stuck there forever, too, until they have the fantastic idea of escaping in Bing Bong's song-powered rocket!

Trunk holds top hat in place

Rainbow rocket trail

Getting Back to Headquarters

With Riley's Islands of Personality crumbling, Joy is desperate to return to Headquarters to put things right. But it's no easy journey! First she loses Sadness and then she gets stuck in the Memory Dump with Bing Bong. It will take brains, bravery and more than a little luck to get back!

Bing Bong's song-powered rocket

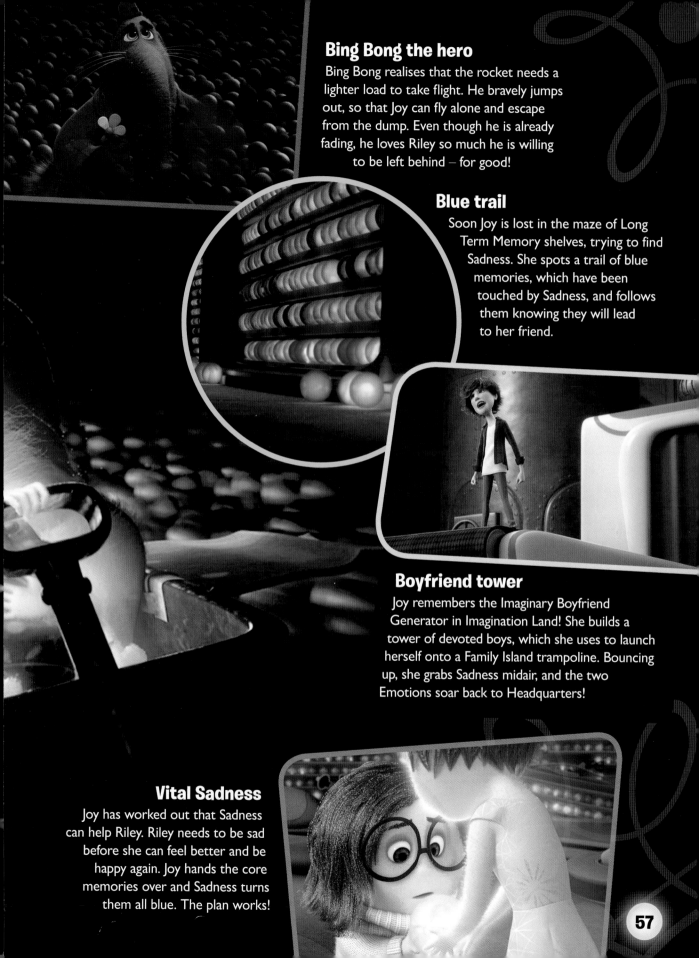

Bing Bong the hero

Bing Bong realises that the rocket needs a lighter load to take flight. He bravely jumps out, so that Joy can fly alone and escape from the dump. Even though he is already fading, he loves Riley so much he is willing to be left behind – for good!

Blue trail

Soon Joy is lost in the maze of Long Term Memory shelves, trying to find Sadness. She spots a trail of blue memories, which have been touched by Sadness, and follows them knowing they will lead to her friend.

Boyfriend tower

Joy remembers the Imaginary Boyfriend Generator in Imagination Land! She builds a tower of devoted boys, which she uses to launch herself onto a Family Island trampoline. Bouncing up, she grabs Sadness midair, and the two Emotions soar back to Headquarters!

Vital Sadness

Joy has worked out that Sadness can help Riley. Riley needs to be sad before she can feel better and be happy again. Joy hands the core memories over and Sadness turns them all blue. The plan works!

Mixed Emotions

Joy and Sadness have pretty different ways of looking at things. In fact, Joy has always wondered why Sadness was in Headquarters at all. Surely she doesn't do anything good for Riley? However, Joy is soon astonished to discover that Sadness has an important role to play in Riley's mind after all!

Care and share
When Sadness first arrived in Headquarters, Joy had to get used to sharing the controls. Since then she has tried to keep Sadness out of the way so that Riley stays happy.

Touch of Sadness
After Sadness touches a happy memory it turns sad and blue! This makes Joy sure that Sadness only hurts Riley. Why can't Sadness just control herself and stay away from the memories!

No fun found

Joy is always trying to encourage Sadness to be happier and "find the fun". But eventually Joy realises that to help Riley, she needs to work with Sadness as a team. Even though Joy may not like it, feeling sad can sometimes be really important for Riley.

A good cry

Joy is surprised to see how talking about being sad helps Bing Bong feel better. Sadness has some other decent ideas, too! Joy starts to appreciate that Sadness might have more to offer Riley than she first thought.

Feeling blue

Sadness is finally in control! She removes the idea bulb so Riley comes home. Then she makes Riley so sad that she tells Mum and Dad how she really feels. The Emotions watch as Riley is hugged by her loving parents. The Andersens can get through this together!

Growing Up

As Riley turns 12-years-old, she begins to feel more settled in San Francisco. She is growing up fast, with new interests and a different view of the world. Coping with the move has also given Riley a more grown-up attitude. But despite all the changes, the Emotions are thrilled to see that underneath she is still the same Riley!

Hockey fans
Riley joins a new ice hockey team based in San Francisco. Her parents are there to support her at every game, though their painted faces can be a little embarrassing. Go Foghorns!

Expanded console
Riley growing up brings a whole new set of challenges for the Emotions. Fortunately, they have a brand new upgraded and expanded console to keep everything under control!

OUCH

SAFETY HAT

Happy again

Soon Riley is back to her normal happy self! She has a new set of friends, loves her new (furnished!) house, and is playing ice hockey again! Although she still has fond memories of Minnesota, now Riley is excited about her life in San Francisco.

Which Emotion are You?

Answer each of the following questions by picking one answer. Write down the letter of the one you choose.

Working in Headquarters is not an easy job. You have to have your wits about you and make very quick decisions. Imagine you were one of the Emotions for a day. Which one would you be most like? Would you share Joy's sunny outlook or feel furious like Anger? Take the quiz to find out!

1. Riley just scored a fantastic ice hockey goal. How do you feel?

A. Yaaaaay! I feel on top of the world!

B. Why doesn't Riley score more goals like that any more?

C. NEVER MIND THE GOAL! THAT GIRL TRIED TO TRIP RILEY UP!

D. Honestly, that goalkeeper's outfit is SO not cool...

E. Oh no, the other team is going to be very angry!

2. Mum serves "broccoli surprise" for lunch, with a side dish of broccoli and a thick topping of broccoli sauce. What is your first reaction?

A. Let's give it a try! At least it's healthy!

B. Oh no! Mum doesn't love Riley anymore!

C. WHAT? BROCCOLI? I'M GOING TO EXPLODE!

D. I think I'm going to be sick!

E. This is the start of something really creepy...

3. In order to make Riley laugh, Dad starts acting silly in the kitchen making gorilla noises. How do you react?

A. You laugh! Dad is a seriously funny guy!

B. Woah! Gorillas are an endangered species! Sniff sniff!

C. ARE YOU SAYING RILEY LOOKS LIKE A BIG HAIRY GORILLA, CLEVER CLOGS?

D. This is **SO** embarrassing! Check the windows for any passing cool kids!

E. Is something weird going on? Dad usually makes monkey sounds, not gorilla noises…

4. Mum and Dad take Riley out for a day exploring downtown San Francisco. How do you feel looking around this amazing city?

A. Fantastic! This is the perfect family day out!

B. Utterly miserable! San Francisco has such a depressing fog that spoils the view.

C. **I AM LIVID!** Call this a day out? This place is too hilly and far too busy!

D. Embarrassed! Mum and Dad are treating Riley like she's about five years old!

E. Run away! Downtown is full of hairy, scary, man-eating monsters! Isn't it?

5. It's the day Riley's best friend Meg is coming all the way from Minnesota to visit San Francisco. What's the first thing you do in the morning?

A. Feel very excited. Today is going to be amazing!

B. Worry about the overwhelming despair Riley will feel when Meg has to leave.

C. Make a list of things you're annoyed with Meg about. She should call more!

D. Prepare a disaster plan just in case Meg is carrying infectious diseases.

E. Feel very nervous. What if Meg and Riley don't get along any more?

Check your answers!

Mostly As:
You're most like **Joy**. You're optimistic and always looking on the bright side!

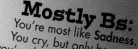

Mostly Bs:
You're most like **Sadness**. You cry, but only because you're thoughtful and sensitive. You know what's important.

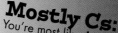

Mostly Cs:
You're most like **Anger**. You're furious because you demand fairness! You always stand up for yourself.

Mostly Ds:
You're most like **Disgust**. You steer clear of what you don't like. You know your mind and keep healthy.

Mostly Es:
You're most like **Fear**. The world might be scary to you, but you always stay safe and keep out of danger.

Acknowledgements

DK | Penguin Random House

Project Editor Lisa Stock
Designers Chris Gould, Anna Pond
Senior Designer Lynne Moulding
Pre-Production Producers Siu Chan, Jenny Murray
Senior Producer Alex Bell
Managing Editor Sadie Smith
Managing Art Editor Ron Stobbart
Art Director Lisa Lanzarini
Publisher Julie Ferris
Publishing Director Simon Beecroft

First published in Great Britain in 2015 by
Dorling Kindersley Limited
80 Strand, London WC2R 0RL
A Penguin Random House Company

15 16 17 18 19 10 9 8 7 6 5 4 3 2
005–259634–May/2015

A CIP catalogue record for this book
is available from the British Library.

ISBN: 978-0-2411-8679-4

Printed and bound in Slovakia

DK would like to thank Steve Bynghall for his writing, Lauren Nesworthy and Julia March for
their editorial assistance, and Chelsea Alon, Laura Uyeda, Kelly Bonbright, Scott Tilley, Winnie
Ho, Danny Saeva, and Roxanna Ashton at Disney Publishing.

A WORLD OF IDEAS:
SEE ALL THERE IS TO KNOW

www.dk.com
www.disney.com